# Harry's Dog

Chris Inman



Cornelsen

**Harry's Dog**
Chris Inman

*Übungen zu den Texten*
Prof. Dr Liesel Hermes

*Umschlaggestaltung*
Heike Börner, dia

*Titelbilder*
Corel Library

*Illustration*
Roy Schofield

*Technische Umsetzung*
Saskia Klemm

**www.cornelsen.de**

1. Auflage, 10. Druck 2015
Alle Drucke dieser Auflage sind inhaltlich unverändert und können im Unterricht nebeneinander verwendet werden.



Druck: Beltz Bad Langensalza GmbH

ISBN 978-3-464-05949-4

Inhalt gedruckt auf säurefreiem Papier aus nachhaltiger Forstwirtschaft.

## Contents

# Harry's Dog

"Barney, here boy, here!" In the woods outside Hatfield, a big untidy dog stopped and listened.

"Here, Barney, good dog!" Barney barked at* a rabbit, then ran.

Barney found Harry Peel in a field outside the woods. "Good old Barney, good dog," said Harry. "You always come when there's food. Here, let's have lunch." He took two sausages out of his bag, gave the small sausage to Barney and started to eat the other.

Barney was happy about the sausage. Harry was happy, too. He liked going to the woods and fields outside Hatfield with his dog. "Barney is my best friend," he often told Dave King. Dave always answered, "Thanks very much!" and barked at him.

It was the school holidays, the time Harry liked most. There were no other people in the woods. All the adults were at work, and his school friends liked doing things in town or at home. Harry liked doing those things, too. But sometimes it was good to be alone, out in the country, in the sun. Barney wasn't interested in ideas like that. With Harry, he was never alone. Barney was interested in smelly things in the woods and small animals. He tried to catch* them. Harry liked small animals, too. But he knew Barney never caught* them, so that was all right.

Things were only difficult when it was time to go home. Barney never wanted* to go home. He came when Harry shouted*, but then he sat and waited, and didn't move. It was like a game. Harry talked to Barney and shouted, "Come on, home boy." Barney stayed there and didn't move. Then Harry laughed and put him on the lead* and pulled him to the bus stop. Today was different*. When it was time to go, Harry shouted to Barney. But Barney didn't come. He stayed in the woods and barked. "Now what?" thought Harry. "He knows it's time to go home. This is a new game. But I'm not going to play."

"Barney, here boy, now!" shouted Harry. Barney barked six times, but he didn't come. "That dog!" thought Harry. "Well, I'm not going into the woods to look for him for half an hour. Am I his owner or is he my owner? I'd like to know!" And he started walking to the bus stop.

Barney didn't want that, of course, and he came out of the woods and ran after him. Harry caught him and put him on the lead. But Barney ran to the woods again and pulled Harry after him. Harry fell and was very angry.

"Right, that's it," he shouted. "You bad dog! You're going to find out who is the owner, and it isn't you!" And he caught Barney again and carried him to the bus stop.

Barney had other ideas. He didn't want to get on the bus and go home when there was something important in the woods. He barked and tried hard to get away, and Harry almost dropped him. But when the bus left the bus stop, there was a hot*, angry and not very comfortable boy* and a big, noisy dog on it.

Barney and Harry weren't popular on that bus. Barney barked, and Harry said, "Be quiet, Barney," again and again. A man said to Harry, "Listen, young man, I've got an idea. You be quiet." Harry was very surprised*, but he didn't say 'Be quiet, Barney' any more.

"That's good," said the man. "Before, we had your dog's noise *and* your noise. Now we've only got your dog's noise. That's much better."

Then the man looked at Barney and said, "Be quiet, Barney." Barney was quiet.

Poor Harry. He sat there in the bus and tried not to look at the other people.

"Barney," he thought. "My best friend! How can you do this to me?"

When Harry got off the bus, Barney suddenly tried to get away again. Harry dropped him and Barney ran. Harry tried to catch him, but he was too fast.

"Oh well, silly dog," said Harry. "Go home alone, then. But wait till I arrive home. Just wait ...!"

"Are you talking to me?" a woman asked him.

"Oh no, only to my dog," said Harry.

"Poor boy," said the woman to her friend. "He thinks he's talking to a dog, but he hasn't got a dog."

Harry went home, very angry.

When Harry arrived home, Barney wasn't there. "Where can he be?" he asked his mother.

"Oh dear." His mother thought.

And suddenly, he wasn't angry any more. He thought about busy roads and cars and accidents. "Poor Barney," he thought. "Where is he? What can I do?"

When Mr Peel came home from work at the police-station, Barney still wasn't there.

"I can't understand it, Dad," Harry told* his father. "Where can he be? I hope he's all right."

"Tell me everything," said Mr Peel. So Harry told him the story*. "Hmm," said Mr Peel. And he thought for a minute.
"Harry," he said suddenly, "let's go back to the woods."
"To the woods?" answered Harry. "Do you think ...?"
"I don't know," answered Mr Peel. "Let's go and see."

Mr Peel drove Harry to the woods. They walked away from the road. It was quiet everywhere. Then, after five minutes, Harry said, "Hey, I can hear* something. It's Barney. He's barking. Let's go and find him."
Barney found *them*. He ran to Harry and then stopped and barked again. "Barney, Barney, you're all right," shouted Harry. And then "Hey, Barney, stop! Where are you going?"
"Let's go after him," said Mr Peel. They ran after Barney, till suddenly he stopped again and barked and barked and barked.
"Hey, Dad," shouted Harry. "There's a boy here."
"What are you doing here?" he asked the boy. "Are you OK?"
"No, I'm not," answered the boy. "I tried to climb* that tree*, but I fell, and now I can't move. Your dog found me this afternoon. He left me for a time, but then he came back and waited here with me. He's a lovely dog."
"Hmm, that looks like a broken leg*, young man," said Mr Peel. "But I think you're going to be all right now. Thanks to Barney here. Good dog, Barney. Good boy. Now, I've got my police radio here, so I can ask for help. You need to get to hospital. Fast."
"Good dog, Barney," said Harry. "You wanted to tell me, but I didn't understand. Hey! Where are you going?" Barney ran into the woods.
He came back with a very small rabbit. "Oh Barney, no," said Harry. Barney looked at him, then at Mr Peel.
"No, Barney," said Mr Peel.
"You can have a sausage at home," said Harry.

"Three sausages," said Mr Peel. But it was too late. Barney barked. He was happy again.

And that's the end of the story – almost. Except for one thing: the boy's father told the newspaper. And the next week, there was the story, on page 1, next to a big picture of Harry and Barney, the "Heroes* of Hatfield". Barney ate the newspaper.

p. 4 bark at (v) = *anbellen;* catch, caught (v) = *fangen, fing;*
want (v) = *wollen;* shout (v) = *rufen;*
put on the lead = *an die Leine nehmen;* different = *anders*
p. 5 hot = *erhitzt;* a not very comfortable boy = *ein Junge, der sich sehr unbehaglich fühlte;* surprised = *überrascht*
p. 6 told (v) = *erzählte*
p. 7 story = *Geschichte;* hear (v) = *hören;*
climb (v) = *klettern auf;* tree = *Baum;*
broken leg = *gebrochenes Bein*
p. 8 hero = *Held/in*

# Simon's New Uniform

"Simon Best, just look at your uniform! You can't come to school like that."

"Yes, Mr Pitt, – erm – no, Mr Pitt," answered Simon. He looked at his uniform. It *was* dirty, no question about that. "Not blue, more blue and brown," he thought. "But you can't play football without goalposts*."

He didn't say that to Mr Pitt, because Mr Pitt was angry.

"Come here, Simon," he said. "Oh look at your trousers, boy! You've got half a field on them. And the other half is on your shoes! You're making everything dirty. Does your mother know? When did she see your uniform? Well, say something, Simon. Answer me. Don't just stand there!"

"My mother saw me this morning," he said.

"But that was before the football game," he thought.

"And you played football on the way to school* this morning, right?" said Mr Pitt. "OK, Simon, you can stay. I'm not going to send you home. But only because you'd like to go home. Go back to your place. You can sit on your chair, but don't touch it with your trousers."

The class laughed at the joke. Mr Pitt wasn't often angry, but it was always fun.

"Simon Best, just look at your uniform! You can't come into the house like that."

"Oh, Mum," said Simon.

"No, stay there in the garden," said Mrs Best. "Leave your shoes in the garage. You can clean them this evening. Now give me your clothes."

"Mum!" said Simon.

"Give me them!" said his mother. "You aren't going to bring all that mud into the house. And how often have I got to tell you? Your school uniform clothes aren't goalposts. They're too expensive."

Mrs Best took Simon's clothes and she put them in the basket.
"OK," said Mrs Best. "You can come in now. But go and have a bath. *Now*, Simon, no questions, no buts!"
Simon went.

Mr Best arrived home. He looked at all Simon's dirty clothes in the wash basket and said, "Goalposts again?"
"Goalposts again," said Simon's mother. "Or, I don't know, perhaps his trousers were the ball. That boy and football."
"Hmm," said Mr Best. "But, you know, it isn't so bad. He needs some new uniform clothes. These here are too small for him. They look old, too."
Mrs Best didn't look happy. School uniforms cost lots of money. But she said, "OK. Let's take him to town on Saturday morning and buy him a new uniform."
"Saturday morning?" said Simon, that evening. "Oh no! I'm playing football on Saturday morning. It's important. The youth club team is practising. I can't miss* that."

"I'm sorry, Simon," answered his father, "but you've got to have some new uniform clothes. We can't go in the week because your mum and I are at work. We can't go on Saturday afternoon because Uncle Steve is coming for a visit, so it has got to be Saturday morning."

"But Dad, I can't miss ..."

"Simon, I saw Mr Dalglish from the youth club yesterday. He told me you're the best player in the team. You play football almost every day on the way to school *and* on the way home. You practise so much, I'm sure you can miss one match. I can phone Mr Dalglish tomorrow and explain."

Simon was angry now. "Dad, I don't need any school uniform. Uniform is silly. It's OK for small children, but I'm too old for it now. I don't *want* a uniform. I can go to school in my jeans and pullover."

"Please don't be silly, Simon. You know you've got to wear uniform to school. All the pupils have got to, so why not you? Now be quiet. I'm tired after work and I want to read the newspaper."

Simon went to his room to listen to some CDs. "Uniform, uniform," he thought. "Who needs it? But I'm not going to miss the game on Saturday and I'm not going to have a silly new uniform."

Saturday morning was sunny. A lovely April day. But cold, very cold. And at half past six, Simon Best left the house. He had all his football things in a bag and some sandwiches for his breakfast.

His parents and his sister, Pat, were still asleep, of course. "They're going to be surprised," thought Simon.

"And angry, too," said Mr Dalglish at the youth club just before the game. "You aren't going to be very popular."

"Popular?" answered Simon. "I just want to be warm! Two and a half hours outside the youth club on a cold morning! Brrr! Please, Mr Dalglish, let's start the game."

The game was good, and Simon enjoyed it. He played well, too. Well, he needed to run hard to stay warm. But at eleven o'clock the game finished, and the others started to go home. "Now what?" said Simon to his best friend, Frank. "I can't go home now. Uncle Steve is coming at two o'clock, so there's still time to go and buy a new uniform before that. But I don't want to wait here another two hours. It's too cold!"

"Come home with me," answered Frank. "I've got that super new CD by the Boring Teachers. Let's listen to that. You can have lunch with us, too."

"Oh great!" Simon was very happy. "But I can only stay till half past one. I don't want to miss Uncle Steve. He always does something nice with us."

"The Boring Teachers are great," said Simon. "I'd like to get that CD, but I haven't got the money. And I can't ask mum or dad. Not after this morning. They're going to be too angry."

"Why not ask your Uncle Steve?" said Frank.

"Hey, great idea!" said Simon. "He always buys us something. Bye, Frank. Got to go! I mustn't miss him!"

Simon arrived home at twenty to two. Just then, his father came in from the garden. "Oh, hi, Simon. There you are."

"Er – hi Dad," said Simon, and went red. "I er – went to the youth club to play football."

"Mm. That's what I thought," answered his father, and laughed.

"Where are mum and Pat?" Simon asked.

"Oh, they're in town with Uncle Steve," said Mr Best. "He arrived at one o'clock. They're at the cinema. They're going to see that new film. You know. Pat told us about it last week."

"Oh, no!" said Simon. "Oh, but Dad! I wanted to see that film, too."

"Oh dear," said his father. "Oh yes, I remember that now. But you see, Simon, the film starts at two o'clock, and you came back so late from football."

Simon just stood there. He felt terrible. No film, no Uncle Steve, no Boring Teachers CD. What an afternoon!

"Poor old Simon," said Mr Best. "Come on, let's do something, just you and me, eh? Let's go into town, too. I can buy you a new school uniform."

p.9 goalpost = *Torpfosten*;
on the way to school = *auf dem Schulweg*
p.10 miss (v) = *verpassen*

# Guy Fawkes Night*

"Remember, remember the fifth of November," sang* Ann Green one evening at the youth club. "What?" shouted her friends from Park School. "It's only September! It's still summer. Who wants to think about cold, dark November? Not us, thank you very much!"

"Oh, but the fifth," said Ann. "We want a good youth club bonfire* on Guy Fawkes Night. Remember last year. We started too late and we didn't find enough* wood*. The five-minute bonfire, that was us. And didn't we look silly! A Guy Fawkes party and everybody was cold."

"Hmm, yes," said Liz Dean. "That's right. We don't want that again. I've got an idea. Let's have a picnic out in the old woods on Saturday. We can enjoy the warm weather and collect wood for the bonfire."

"Saturday?" said Simon Best. "Oh no, not Saturday. I'm ..."

"Yes, yes, we all know," said his sister, Pat. "You're playing football on Saturday. But you can come in the afternoon."

On Saturday afternoon, the members of the youth club found lots of wood. They worked hard and collected enough for a big bonfire. "This is good," said Sam Cooper. "Now we don't need to find any more wood before November."

"Oh, we can always use more wood," said the others. "You just don't want to work, Sam."

"Hey, I've just thought of something," said Liz.

"Wow," answered Dave King. "That's the first time this year. How did you do that?" Everybody laughed.

"All right, all right," said Liz, her face red. "You can laugh. Now answer this question. How are we going to take all this wood back to the youth club?"

"Oh," said the others, and they stood and looked at the wood.

“I know,” said Dave. “Let’s walk back. Then we can all carry some of the wood.”

“Oh, yeah,” said Harry. “Any more great ideas? OK. We leave the wood here, and our dads can fetch it by car tomorrow. Right?”

“The next thing we need,” said somebody at the youth club, “is a guy*.”

“And some money for fireworks*, don’t forget,” said Sam. “Let’s make our guy and then take him into town. We can ask people for a penny for the guy.”

“A penny?” laughed Harry. “How many fireworks do you want to buy? One? We need pounds.”

“Yeah, that’s right, Harry,” answered the others, “but it’s silly. Who is going to give us so much money?”

It was a good guy. They all thought that. “He’s worth a pound,” said Harry. “Let’s try.”

The first evening, Ann and Liz took the guy into town. “So that’s three into town,” said the bus driver.

“Three?” asked Ann, surprised. “No. Only two.”

“What about him?” asked the driver.

“Who?” asked Ann. “Oh him. But that’s our guy.”

“I’m not interested in his name,” answered the driver. “He needs a ticket.”

“A ticket? For a guy? But ...”

“Listen,” said the driver. “Can he stand?”

“No, of course he can’t stand.”

“Then he needs a seat*, so he needs a ticket.”

Liz and Ann gave the driver the money and carried the guy to a seat in the bus. He looked very good on his seat next to Ann, and she started to talk to him.

“Now listen, Guy,” she said. “Don’t lose your ticket. And don’t forget, you’ve got to collect money for us. You mustn’t cost money.”

The next evening, Harry and Dave took the guy into town. They found a good place in the town centre. It was near the station, and lots of people went past.

"A pound for the guy," shouted Harry. "Fifty pence for the guy," shouted Dave. "Or twenty ... or ten ..."

Most people just walked past. But enough people gave money. In one hour, Harry and Dave collected £3.50. They were very happy. Then, suddenly, a policeman came along.

"What are you doing here?" he asked. "You can't collect money in the town centre! What are your names?"

"My name is  Harry, Dad," said Harry.

"Right, Mr Harry," said Mr Peel, and he tried not to laugh. "You've got to go. And take Mr Fawkes with you. I'm going to come back in two hours. Don't be here!" And he walked away.

November 5th was a cold, dry* day. "Just right for fireworks," said Ann. "Wet weather is no good, you can't see things."

"Ann," said Miss May, "perhaps you can talk to your neighbour* about Maths, not bonfire weather, OK? You're still in school just now. Your bonfire party is this evening."
"Sorry, Miss May," said Ann. But she wasn't sorry, and not many pupils thought about their school work that day.

In the evening, the members of the youth club all came with their parents and brothers and sisters. Almost every house had a bonfire in the garden, and the noise and light of fireworks was everywhere. But the bonfire at the youth club was better than all the others, and there were more fireworks.
There were sausages and other things to eat at the bonfire, and everybody ate and watched and shouted at the fireworks. The children were very excited* and happy.
Suddenly, Sam Cooper shouted, "Oh no, don't do that!" Then there was the noise of a firework and another funny* noise, like a small explosion.
"Ow, ow, ow, that hurts*," shouted somebody. Sam Cooper ran up to his mother.
"Come and help, Mum," he said. "It's our Mark. He put a firework in a bottle. I shouted at him, but it was too late. The bottle broke and now he has got some glass in his knee*."
Mr Peel went with Mrs Cooper and Sam to find Mark.
"Ow," said Mark again. "My knee hurts!"
"Well, of course it hurts," said his mother. "You're a very very silly boy. Why did you put a firework in a bottle? Sometimes I don't understand you boys!"
"I wanted to see something different," said Mark.
"Well," said Mr Peel, and he laughed. "You saw something different, and you felt* something different. I hope you learned something different, too." He pulled the glass out of Mark's knee.
"Ooooowwww," shouted Mark

Suddenly, Mrs Best shouted, "Oh no, no!"
"Oh dear, now what?" said Mr Peel, and he ran to Mrs Best. "Is everybody all right?" he asked. And then, surprised, "Why is everybody laughing?"
"Look," shouted Mrs Best. "Look at the guy. What is it wearing?" Mr Peel looked at the guy.
"I'm not sure ... yes, the guy is wearing school uniform. What a good idea."

p. 14 Guy Fawkes Night = *Am 5. November 1605 wurde Guy Fawkes, Anführer einer Gruppe von Verschwörern, bei dem Versuch entdeckt, das britische Parlament und den König, James I., mit riesigen Mengen Schießpulver in die Luft zu sprengen. König und Parlament wurden gerettet, Guy Fawkes und seine Mitverschwörer hingerichtet. Noch heute feiern die Briten den 5. November mit Feuerwerk und Freudenfeuern, auf denen Guy-Fawkes-Puppen verbrannt werden;*
sang (v) = *sang;* bonfire = *Freudenfeuer;* enough = *genug;* wood = *Holz*
p. 15 guy = *Puppe;* fireworks = *Feuerwerkskörper;* seat = *Sitzplatz*
p. 16 dry = *trocken*
p. 17 neighbour = *Nachbar/in;* excited = *aufgeregt;* funny = *komisch;* hurt (v) = *weh tun;* knee = *Knie;* you felt (v) = *du fühltest*

# Christmas* in England

Christmas in England! Verena wasn't sure now.

"I thought it was a good idea in summer," said Verena to Linda, her English friend, at Linda's house in Paderborn. "And Sam is very nice, of course. I'd like to see him again. But Christmas ... without Mum and Dad, and my grandma. You know, Linda, we Germans always spend Christmas with our families."

"Well, it's the same in England," said Linda. "And you were very happy about the idea in summer, don't you remember?"

"Yes, but ... Oh, I don't know," she said. "It isn't just my family – they're going to miss me. There's ... Oh, English food is so terrible. I can't eat dry cheeseburgers and wet chips for Christmas! And I've got to speak English for two weeks. And ..."

"Verena Siebert!" said Linda, angry now. "You know very well English food is *not* terrible. When did you get cheeseburgers and chips at our house, wet or dry? And English Christmas turkey* is great. Sam can speak *some* German, too. You've got to go. It's too late to say no."

That was two weeks ago. And of course, Verena didn't say no. She flew to London on 17th December. Sam Cooper, his mother and his two brothers met her at the airport. Sam was fun, just like in summer, and there was so much to do. She met his friends from Park School at the youth club, and they all went swimming and then to the cinema. After the film, they bought fish and chips and ate them in the cold street out of some newspaper.

"Why are English chips so wet?" Verena asked Dave King. But Dave didn't understand, and Verena didn't explain. Verena was happy when Liz Dean's dog Snoopy came to meet them. Snoopy liked wet chips.

The next day, Harry Peel's dad had a free day, so he took Harry and Sam and Verena to London. They saw the Christmas lights in Oxford Street and Regent Street. Everything about London was interesting. So many people from so many countries. Before the lights, Mr Peel took them to a restaurant. The owners were black people like Harry and his dad. The food was very different, and Verena enjoyed it. "Much better than wet chips without mayonnaise," she said to Sam.

At half past four on Christmas Eve*, Verena was standing next to the Christmas tree. Sam came into the room.
"Where are your mum and your brothers, Sam?" she asked.
"Oh, mum is still at work," he answered, "and Mark and John are at the supermarket. Mum asked them to buy something at the last minute."
"But it's Christmas Eve," said Verena.
"Yeah," answered Sam. "Isn't that super! There's always something good on TV. Let's make some sandwiches and then we can watch."

"Sandwiches? On Christmas Eve?"

"Well, I can fetch a pizza or some chips," said Sam.

"No, no. Sandwiches are fine," said Verena. "Please, please, *don't* fetch any chips!" she thought. "Oh dear, sandwiches, pizza, chips? What did Linda tell me? English Christmas food is super? And poor Mrs Cooper! Why has she got to work all day on Christmas Eve? I can ask Sam."

But Sam was busy. "Let's hurry up with the sandwiches," he said. "There's a great programme in five minutes."

The programme *was* great, and Verena and Sam laughed and laughed. At the end, Mrs Cooper and the other boys came in. "Good," thought Verena. "Now we can start Christmas and I can give everybody my presents. I hope they like them."

Mrs Cooper made some more sandwiches, and sat with them to watch TV. Verena waited ... and waited. She looked at the Christmas tree. There were no presents there. She looked at Sam and his family. They were all interested in the TV programme. She tried to say something. "Shh, listen," said Sam. "This is the best part."

Seven o'clock. The programme finished. "Good," thought Verena. "Now I can ask Sam." But Sam ran out to the toilet. "The next programme is even better!" he said. Mrs Cooper and Sam's brothers went to make some more sandwiches. Then everybody came back to watch the next programme. Verena wasn't just lonely* now. She was angry, too. And she got up and went to her room.

She came back with her presents for Sam and his family and said, "Happy Christmas." Then she gave everybody a present. The Coopers looked very, very surprised. They even forgot the TV programme. Mrs Cooper spoke first. "Thank you, Verena. That's lovely. It's very nice of you, but ..."

"But, Verena," said Sam. "It isn't Christmas here today. Christmas is tomorrow. Today is only Christmas Eve."

"*Only* Christmas Eve?" said Verena. Now *she* was surprised.

"Only? Christmas Eve is very important. Christmas Eve *is* Christmas. We give everybody presents and sing and ..."

"Oh dear, Verena," said Mrs Cooper. "I'm sorry. In England, we do all that tomorrow, on Christmas Day. Christmas Eve isn't very important here. Is it different in Germany?"

"Oh," said Verena. "Oh, yes, it is, very different."

And suddenly she understood. "But ... Oh well," and Verena laughed. "I'm going to enjoy an English Christmas. Let's put those presents by the tree. But I've got one question."

"What's that?" asked Sam.

"English Christmas food. It isn't sandwiches or chips or ...

"Oh, no," said Sam. "Of course not. English Christmas food is super. There's turkey and there's ..."

Just then, Mark came in. "Telephone for you, Verena," he said. "It's your mum."

"Frohe Weihnachten," said Verena's mother on the phone. Verena was happy again. She spoke to everybody in her family for twenty minutes. "And we're going to eat turkey tomorrow," she finished.

"Now, Sam," she said. "Where's the turkey?"

"The turkey?" said Sam. "Don't you know? It's in ... Well, I can show you. Come in here. It's on the table. There."

And there was the turkey in a great big dish on the table. Well, most of it was in the dish. But some of it was in a large and happy black cat, asleep on the table.

"Oh, Sooty," said Sam. "Oh, no! Mum, help!"

"Oh dear, Sam," said Verena. "I'm sure it was a lovely turkey. English Christmas food is great. But perhaps we can have cheeseburgers and chips?"

p.19 Christmas = *Weihnachten;* turkey = *Truthahn*
p.20 Christmas Eve = *Heiligabend*
p.21 lonely = *einsam*

## No Kittens* in this Flat!

"Sooty is suddenly very big," said Sam Cooper to his friend, Dave King, and pointed to the Cooper family's cat. "Perhaps he eats too much."

"Don't be silly," said Dave. "She's going to have kittens."

"What?" answered Sam. "Don't you be silly. Sooty is a he, not a she. He can't have kittens."

"Oh, well," laughed Dave. "Let's wait and see who is right. But I'm sure – er – he isn't getting too much to eat."

Another two weeks, and Sam knew who was right. "Aaaaagh, oh no!" shouted his mother one evening. Sam and his brothers ran into her room. Sooty was on Mrs Cooper's bed – with four kittens.

"Oh, aren't they lovely!" said Sam.

"Oh, yes, aren't they sweet!" said his brothers.

"Lovely?" said their mother. "Sweet? Just look at my bed! Look at it! And everything was clean this morning."

Sam looked. The bed wasn't clean now, that was for sure*. There was something dark and wet on it, and it was smelly, too. But the bed wasn't important. The important thing was the kittens, and they were lovely. Poor Sam. He said that to his mother – and that wasn't a good idea.

"Not important?" she shouted. "Not important? Now, listen to me, Sam Cooper. How am I going to get this bed clean? Tell me that. And where am I going to sleep tonight*? Would you like to sleep here? Can I have your bed?"

"Er – well ...," said Sam.

"Hm. I was right," said his mother. "Well, here's something you can think about. What are we going to do with them? One cat in the flat is too much. I'm not going to have five. No! No kittens in this flat!"

"Oh, Mum," said Sam, Mark and John.

"You can say 'Oh, Mum' from now till breakfast time. I said 'no kittens,' and I mean 'no kittens.' I'm going to take them to the vet* tomorrow."
"Oh, no! Mum! You can't," shouted the boys.
"Quiet! One more word and Sooty can go, too. He ate the turkey at Christmas, and now he's using my bed as ..."
"Er – Mum, Sooty is not a he any more, he's a she," said Sam.
"Sa-a-am," said his mother. "Just one more word, that's all.

One more ..." Sam was quiet. "That's better," said Mrs Cooper. "Now take these cats out of here. Put them all in Sooty's basket and then go to bed."
Sam and his brothers didn't sleep that night. They felt terrible. Those four lovely kittens. And Mum wanted to take them to the vet. The boys knew why.

"Mum," said Sam in the morning. "Please. You mustn't take them to the vet. We can find homes for them."
"All right, Sam," said Mrs Cooper, and she laughed. "Things look better this morning. I had a comfortable night on the sofa. OK. But they aren't going to stay here. Kittens need their mother for six weeks. So you've got six weeks to find homes for them. After that, they go."
Sam felt much better. Six weeks. That was lots of time. And the kittens were so lovely. "I'm sure all my friends would like one," he thought. "This is going to be easy."

He tried Dave King first. "Dave, would you like a kitten?"
"A kitten?" answered Dave. "But you haven't got any kittens. You can't have. Sooty is a he. He just eats too much."
"OK, OK, you were right," answered Sam. "So would you like a kitten?"
"Yes please," said Dave. Sam felt very happy. But then Dave said, "You know my sister Sally? Well, she has got some fish. She loves her silly fish, too. But cats eat fish, right? And then big sisters eat young brothers. And that's me. Sorry, Sam. I can't help you."
"Oh well," thought Sam. "I've got other friends." And he phoned Ann Green.
"Kittens?" said Ann. "Oh, how lovely. I'd like to have a kitten."
"Great," said Sam. "There are four. You can have ..."
"But there's my dog," said Ann.
"Oh, that's all right," said Sam. "Lots of people have a cat *and* a dog."
"You don't understand, Sam," answered Ann. "Billy is frightened of cats."
"Frightened?" Sam almost shouted. "Is that a joke? Dogs aren't frightened of cats."
"This dog is," said Ann. "Sorry, Sam."

"Oh dear," thought Sam. "Perhaps this is going to be difficult. I know. I can ask Liz Dean. She has got a dog, too – but Snoopy is OK."

"Do you like cats, Liz?" asked Sam.

"I love them," said Liz. "And kittens are so sweet."

"Great!" said Sam. "I'd like to give you a kitten. I've got four."

"Oh, but Sam, don't forget Snoopy."

"Snoopy? Why? Is he frightened of cats, like Ann's dog?"

"Don't be silly, Sam," answered Liz. "Snoopy isn't frightened of cats. He loves them."

"That's OK, then," said Sam. "You can ..."

"For breakfast," finished Liz. "Sorry, Sam."

"Oh, no," thought Sam. "Everybody has got a silly dog."

"What do you think about kittens, Harry," asked Sam when he met Harry Peel.

"Today's kitten is tomorrow's cat," laughed Harry. "But most of the time, I don't think about kittens."

"Harry, please," said Sam. "It's no joke. I've got to find homes for four kittens. Wouldn't you like to have a cat?"

"Yes, I would, Sam, but you see, it's Barney, my dog. He thinks he's my owner. And he's very jealous*. He's angry when I play with other dogs. No, he wouldn't like a cat."

"Harry!" shouted Sam. "It's *no joke!* I told you that. My friends don't want kittens. My brothers' friends don't want kittens, and my mother is going to take them to the vet. I've *got* to find homes for them."

"Sorry, Sam. Hey, listen. I've got an idea. Why don't you put adverts* in shop windows?"

The adverts cost Sam all his pocket-money, but they were worth it. After six weeks, three of the kittens had homes. Only the fourth didn't have a new owner. "Don't forget," said Mrs Cooper to Sam and his brothers. "Tomorrow is the last day. He has got to go."

The kitten walked up to Mrs Cooper and looked at her. It said, "Miaow."
Sam put it on his mother's knee, and it said "Miaow" again. Mrs Cooper looked at it for a long time. Then she looked at Sam. "All right, Sam," she said. "You win. He can stay."
Sam was happy. "Thanks, Mum," he said. "You're great."
"Well," she answered, "you tried very hard. But one thing. Sooty can visit the vet. I don't want any more kittens in this flat." Then suddenly, she shouted, "Hey, what's this? My skirt is all wet! Oh no! Sam Cooper, take this cat away and put it in the basket, now!" And she ran out of the room.
Sam took the kitten to the basket and tried not to laugh.

p. 23 kitten = *Kätzchen;* that was for sure = *das stand fest;* tonight = *heute Nacht*
p. 24 vet = *Tierarzt/ärztin*
p.26 jealous = *eifersüchtig;* advert = *Annonce*

# Easter* in the Country

"Easter is next weekend," said Mr Best. "Four days without work. I'm going to enjoy that."

"Four days!" laughed Pat. "Poor old dad. We get fourteen days with no school. But school is different from an office. We've got to work hard there."

"One more joke like that, young Pat, and we can all stay at home next weekend," said her father. "No trip to Hutton, I don't have to drive for miles and miles. Your mum and I can do what *we* want to do, and you and Simon can learn some more Maths and German. How's that?"

"Aw, Dad," said Pat. "Come on! You and mum want to go to Hutton, too. You know that. You always say you need a holiday in the country."

"I need three or four holidays in the country," laughed her father. "But three or four days on the Ogdens' farm is all I'm going to get."

Up in Hutton-le-Hole, Jill Ogden was happy about the Bests' visit, too. "When are they going to arrive on Friday?" she asked her mother.

"Oh, about eleven o'clock," said Mrs Ogden. "I talked to Mrs Best on the phone last night. She says they want to start very early* in the morning to miss* the holiday traffic jams*. You can make some hot cross buns*, and we can eat them when they arrive."

"Mmm, super idea," said Jill. "They're going to be hungry after the long trip."

"Yes," said her mother. "And I don't want to give Pat supermarket cakes again, like last time."

The Bests didn't arrive till three o'clock. Mr and Mrs Best looked tired. They came into the house and fell into the comfortable chairs. The buns were cold now, but everybody

enjoyed them. Pat and Simon weren't tired. They went out to help Jill and Mr Ogden with the animals.
"Why are you so late?" asked Jill.
"Oh, there was a traffic jam for thirty miles, and that took four hours," answered Pat. "Boring. But it's great to be here again."
"Your parents look terrible," said Jill.
"Yes, poor mum and dad. It was very hot in the car, and they've got headaches*."
"That's right," said Simon. "A long journey is hard when you're old. And dad is thirty-eight. Adults don't have much fun."

The Easter weather stayed warm and sunny, and Pat spent all Saturday outside with Jill. They got up at six o'clock and took the animals out to the fields. Pat helped Jill to look after her horse, and even tried to ride it. "Next time," said Jill, "you can stay for a week or two. Then you can learn to ride." After that, they went to different parts of the farm and did small jobs for Mr Ogden.
Simon wasn't with them. He found some boys in the village and went to play football with them. Pat was happy about that. "I like my brother," she told Jill. "And I like him most when he isn't there."

In the afternoon, Pat and Jill gave the chickens* their food. One big red chicken took the food from Pat's hand.
"She's lovely," said Pat. "I'm going to call her Caroline."
"Oh, I don't like to give the chickens names," said Jill.
"Why not?" asked Pat.
But Jill just said, "Come on, let's go and collect the eggs. I always like doing that. You put your hand under the chickens and the eggs are so warm."
"We're going to get some different eggs tomorrow," said Pat. "Easter Sunday and Easter eggs. I love it."

"Mmm, and we have a great big Easter Sunday lunch, and my dad doesn't work so much. I always enjoy Easter," answered Jill.

On Easter Sunday morning there were chocolate Easter eggs for the children – and for some of the adults, too. "I bought an egg for you in London," said Pat and Simon's mother to Mrs Ogden, and gave her a lovely big box.

"Thank you," said Jill's mother. "When I was a girl like Jill, I loved chocolate Easter eggs, and I still love them now. But I don't often get them." And she looked at Mr Ogden.
He only said, "You get enough eggs from your chickens."
"Hmmh," said Mrs Ogden. "You men ..." and then she stopped, surprised. "What's this?" she said, and pulled a funny brown thing out of the box. Then she started to laugh. "You town people have funny ideas about eggs. They aren't like this, you know. Or are the chickens different in the city?"
Mrs Best went red. "Oh dear," she said. "Oh no! It was so hot in the car on Friday. And the eggs were in the sun, and ... Oh dear, I didn't think!"

"Oh, well," laughed Mrs Ogden. "Let's call it a modern art egg. Mmmmm. The chocolate is still very good. Oh, and you children!" She looked at Simon. "Don't eat all your eggs now. Remember. We're going to have a big Easter Sunday lunch."

At one o'clock, the two families were at the table for lunch.
"All this food," said Pat. "It's almost like Christmas."
"I'm not hungry," said Simon. "Can I go and watch TV?"
"Are you ill, Simon?" asked his mother.
"No, he isn't," said Pat. "He ate four chocolate Easter eggs."
"Aha, I see," said Mr Best. "Yes, Simon. You can watch. You can sit right there and watch us. We're going to eat lunch."
Simon looked at Pat. "Girls!" he said. And then, "Sisters!"
Everybody except Simon started to enjoy the food. Suddenly, Pat asked, "Where was Caroline this morning?"
"Who is Caroline?" asked Mr Ogden.
"Oh, that's my name for one of your chickens," answered Pat. "She's lovely. She ate her food from my hand yesterday. She's red and very big. But I didn't see her this morning."
Mr Ogden didn't say anything. Mrs Ogden didn't say anything. Jill said, "The weather is still lovely. We can go for a long walk this afternoon." Then Pat looked at the chicken on the table. "Oh no!" she shouted. "Oh no! It isn't! It can't be! You didn't ...!" and she ran out of the room.
"Poor Pat," said Jill. "I told her. I don't like to give names to the chickens. But she didn't understand. Oh, well. Happy Easter everybody."

p.28 Easter = *Ostern;* early = *früh;*
miss (v) = *entgehen, vermeiden;* traffic jam = *Verkehrsstau;*
hot cross buns = *Rosinenbrötchen für Karfreitag*
p.29 headache = *Kopfschmerzen;* chicken = *Huhn*

# The Great Africa Sale*

"It's terrible," said Dave King.

"Yes," said his father. "It is."

"But, why doesn't somebody *do* something about it?" asked Dave.

"About what?" answered his father. "Dave, I'm tired after work, and I'm trying to read the newspaper. What are you talking about?"

"Oh, Dad! About the African* children," shouted Dave. "Aren't you watching the TV? There were pictures just now. Hungry children. They can't get enough to eat. They're all going to die*. Thousands and thousands and thousands of them."

"Yes, Dave, I know. It's very bad. Children are dying there all the time. It's always like that in Africa."

"But why, Dad? And why doesn't somebody do something?"

"I'm sorry, Dave, I can't give you an answer," said Mr King. "There are lots of things. There are wars* all the time. They have too many children. They don't work. The weather is too dry. The countries can't buy food because they haven't got enough money. People try to do something. Our country gives money. And there are charities*. They send money and workers, too. But it doesn't help. It's always the same. Every year."

"But I don't understand, Dad. How can they have too many children? All the children die! And how *can* people work when they're hungry all the time? Or when it never rains?"

"Dave, please. I want to read my newspaper. I know it's terrible, I'd like to do something, but I can't. And you can't. It's just too difficult. Now, go and help your mother. She's making something to eat."

Dave was very surprised. His father was a nice man. And he liked explaining things to Dave. So why not this time? He didn't eat tea that evening. He just wasn't hungry.

Dave didn't sleep very much. All night he thought about the TV pictures. "Babies*, little children and people like me and my friends," he thought. "They're all without food, they're all going to die. Thirteen years old, just like me. But they're going to die: today, tomorrow, next week, next month. I've got to do something. But what?"

In the morning, Dave's father said to him, "I wasn't very nice to you yesterday evening, Dave, I'm sorry. But I was very tired. Listen, there was a story in my newspaper about a school in London. The pupils sold old clothes and toys and things. They gave the money to a charity to use in Africa. Perhaps your school can do something like that."
"Thanks, Dad," said Dave. "That's a good idea." And he went off to school.

Dave's friends in Class 2F liked the idea when he told them about it.
"Yeah, I saw that programme," said Harry Peel. "And I felt bad, too. Here we've got too much to eat. We throw food away. There they haven't got enough to eat and the children die. How can that be right? I don't understand it."
"My dad says it's because black people don't want to work," said Pat Best.
"Well," said Harry. "My dad is often very tired when he comes home from the police-station. Do you think he works, perhaps?"
"Oh, Harry," said Pat, and went red. "Oh, Harry, I'm sorry."
Harry laughed. "Your faces*!" he said. "You all look like a wet weekend. Come on! Parents don't know everything. They say silly things sometimes. But we've got work to do. Dave's idea is good. Let's do it."

So, Dave and Harry and their friends in Class 2F started to look for things to sell. They asked friends, they asked neighbours, mothers and fathers, brothers and sisters, aunts and uncles.

"Of course we'd like to help," people always said. "But what do you want?"

"Everything," was the answer. So people gave them everything they didn't want any more. Clothes, toys, things for the house, things for the garden, pictures, books, records and cassettes. Some things were old, some were very old, but some were almost new.

There were other things to do, too, of course. "We've got to tell people about the sale," said Harry. "So we need a date, a time and a place. And we've got to put the things on something, so we need big tables."

"The place is easy," answered Dave. "We're putting everything in our garage, so we can have the sale in our garden. My mum and dad say that's OK."

"Let's ask Mr Hill to lend us some school tables," said Liz Dean. "He'd like to help us."

"Good idea," said Dave. "And Ann, can you make posters for The Great Africa Sale? I can take them to the shops and put them in the windows, and we can put them up in school, too. What about Saturday 24th for a date? That gives us two weeks."

On Friday 23rd June, the friends spent all evening in the Kings' garage. They wanted to get everything ready for the sale. Mr Hill brought some tables in the school van and stayed to help for an hour. Saturday 24th was warm and sunny. They put the tables in the garden and put all the things on them. At two o'clock, everything was ready for The Great Africa Sale, and people started to arrive. Lots of them.

At half past two, there were a hundred people in the Kings' garden.

"This is a very good sale," said Mrs Best's friend, Mrs Sanderson, when they met.

They sold everything. "I'm not surprised," said Harry. "Everything is useful for somebody. What does useful mean? It only means you need a thing now."

That evening, there was a count*-the-money party at Dave's house. Everybody was there.

"Four hundred pounds!" said Dave. "We've got four hundred pounds!" The friends all laughed and shouted. "Who said we can't do anything* for the African people?" shouted Harry. "That money is going to help lots of people."

Mr King sent a cheque for the money to the charity, and the charity sent a letter back to thank Dave and Harry and their friends in Class 2F. Mr Hill put the letter on the wall in school. Dave was very happy. He felt great.

That evening, there was another programme on TV about the hungry children in Africa. "We need about ten million pounds, or these people are going to die," said somebody. Suddenly, Dave didn't feel great any more. "Ten *million* pounds," he thought. "And we sent only four hundred. That isn't going to help. And after all our work." He went to his room and sat on his bed.
His father found him there, and Dave told him about the new programme. Mr King was quiet for a time. Then he said, "You helped somebody, Dave. Because you and your friends had that sale, somebody is not going to die. So don't feel bad just because you can't help all the children. You did something. How many children did I help, when I wanted to read my newspaper?"
Dave tried to feel better. But he didn't sleep very much that night.

p.32 sale = *Basar, Trödelmarkt;* African = *afrikanisch;*
die (v) = *sterben;* war = *Krieg;*
charity = *Wohltätigkeitsorganisation*
p.33 baby = *Säugling, Kleinkind;* face = *Gesicht*
p.35 count (v) = *zählen;* not...anything = *nichts*

# The Class Trip

"Is everybody here?" Mr Hill asked the pupils in the coach.
"No, Mr Hill," answered Harry Peel. "Liz Dean isn't."
"Oh, no! Where is she?" said Mr Hill. "Do you know, Pat?"
"Sorry, Mr Hill, I don't. She was here ten minutes ago. I saw her."
"Well, she isn't here now, and we're all waiting," said Mr Hill.
All the pupils in Class 2F were in the coach outside Park School. It was the best school day of the year, the school day with no school, the day of the class trip. This year, the trip was to Whipsnade Zoo, a big zoo park out in the country, not very far from Hatfield.
All the pupils? Well, almost all. Only Liz Dean wasn't there. And just now, she wasn't a very popular girl. "Oh, why are we waiting, why-y are we waiting?" the class started to sing.
At ten past eight, Mr Hill said, "Oh well, I don't want to go without her, but ..."
Just then, Miss May, the other teacher, said, "Oh, there she is. She's running along the road there. The silly girl wasn't in school at all!"
Liz got into the coach, her face very red. "Sorry, everybody," she said. "I forgot my lunch. I went home again to fetch it."
"Don't be sorry, dear," said the driver. "I enjoyed reading my newspaper for ten more minutes."
"All right, driver, we can go now," said Mr Hill.

It isn't a very long journey from Hatfield to Whipsnade, and the pupils enjoyed it. They sang and talked and were noisy. School was far away.
After half an hour, Miss May got up and said, "Did you all remember to bring two pounds for the tickets? Have the money ready, please. Mr Hill and I are going to collect it now."

When Mr Hill came to Liz Dean, he saw a red face again. "Er – Mr Hill," she said, "I can't find my money. I know I had it. I didn't forget it. But ..."
"It's OK, Liz," laughed Carl, another pupil. "*You* can get into the zoo free, that's for sure! The only question is, are you going to get out again?"
Mr Hill tried to look angry. "Do you want to wait for us all day in the coach, Carl?" he said. And then, "OK, Liz, OK," he said. "Let's just say you're having a bad day. Give me the money tomorrow. I can pay for you now."
The coach stopped outside the zoo, and the excited pupils got out. "Welcome to warm, windy Whipsnade," laughed Miss May.
"Well, we want wet, windy weather, Wiss Way," said Carl. Mr Hill looked very hard* at him, but didn't say a word.

When school classes visit Whipsnade, the zoo looks after them very well. Anna Conder from the information centre came to meet Class 2F and took them over to the centre.
"First, you're going to see a film," she said, "and then some of our young workers are going to come and talk to you. They look after the animals, and you can ask them questions. After that, I'm going to take you to see the baby animals* and tell you more about them."
The class enjoyed the film. "But the best part," said Carl Sweetman at the end, "wasn't the animals. It was Liz Dean." Poor Liz came in late from the toilet, and fell on Miss May when she tried to get past Mr Hill in the dark room.
"Be quiet, Carl," said Mr Hill. "And Liz, please, please try to do everything right now." Liz's face was red again.
The pupils had lots of questions for Anna Conder and the zoo workers. And after the visit to the baby animals, most of them wanted to be zoo workers, too. "But first, I want my lunch," said Harry Peel.

"Me too," said Anna. "And so I'm going to say goodbye. You all go and have lunch now at the picnic tables. This afternoon, Mr Hill and Miss May can show you the other animals. Don't forget to go on our little train to see the African animals. They run free in big fields."

Lunch was happy and noisy. The pupils were excited and had lots to talk about. But suddenly, Ann Green said, "Oh no!" and ran to the teachers.

"What's that on your skirt, Ann?" asked Miss May.

"Wait," said Mr Hill. "Don't tell me ... Liz Dean – right?"

"Well, yes," said Ann, "but, well, Liz wanted to give me some lemonade and then Carl said, 'Look, Liz, there's a rhinoceros* in that tree,' and Liz looked, and all the lemonade went on my skirt."

Mr Hill put his face in his hands.

Miss May said, "Carl, come and see me in school tomorrow, and Liz, please try to be careful*. Ann, I'm sorry, but you've just got to wait for this sunny, windy weather to dry your skirt. It isn't going to take long. Now let's all go to the African train."

The African train was very interesting. A slow trip through fields full of big animals. The animals walked and ran and ate and slept. They weren't interested in the train. They saw it every day.

After the train, Mr Hill said to the class, "OK, you don't need Miss May and me now. Go and look at the animals and meet us at the coach in two hours. We're going to have some coffee. And Liz Dean, please – be careful!"

The pupils were happy without their teachers. There are lots of different animals to see at Whipsnade. Often, the only thing between the animals and the people is a low wall and water*. "Hey, look," said Dave King. "There are great big fish in the water here!"

"Oh where?" said Liz, excited, and ran to look.

Mr Hill wasn't happy when Liz told him. "You dropped your bag in the water because you wanted to see the fish. Is that right?" he asked.

"Yes, Mr Hill," answered Liz, her face red.

"So I've got to find Miss Conder or another zoo worker and ask them to get your bag?"

"Please, Mr Hill," said Liz.

"Liz, can't you even look at fish without dropping bags on them? I'm very angry now. You're a silly girl. You don't look after your things. You forget them, you lose them, you drop them. You come late. You do things first and think second. What can I do with you?"

"I'm sorry, Mr Hill," said Liz. "I'm not usually like this. Today is just one of those days."

"Well, let's hope so," said Mr Hill. "OK, come with me to find Miss Conder. Then be at the coach with the others at half past four."

At twenty-five to five, the coach left the car park to go home to Hatfield. At quarter to five, Miss May said, "But where's Mr Hill? I thought he was at the back."

So the coach went back to Whipsnade. Mr Hill got on. "Sorry everybody. I forgot my bag and all my money in the restaurant. I went back to fetch them, but then I went to the other car park. The coach wasn't there, of course, so I missed ..."

Suddenly Mr Hill stopped. Liz Dean looked very hard at him – and his face went red.

p. 38 hard = *streng;* baby animal = *Jungtier*
p. 39 rhinoceros = *Nashorn*
p. 40 careful = *vorsichtig;* water = *Wasser*

## After the Stories ...

Die meisten Geschichten enthalten Dialoge, d. h. Gespräche zwischen den Personen, die in der Geschichte vorkommen. Geschichten mit Dialogen lassen sich auf unterschiedliche Weise spielen: Man kann sie mit verteilten Rollen lesen, zu einem Hörspiel umschreiben oder als Theaterstück bearbeiten. Ein Hörspiel lässt sich vortragen und auf Kassette aufnehmen. Ein Theaterstück kann in der Klasse vorgespielt oder bei einem Elternabend oder Schulfest aufgeführt werden. Wenn man eine Videokamera zur Verfügung hat, kann man das Theaterstück aufnehmen, einen Film davon herstellen und diesen auch an andere Klassen ausleihen. Alle Geschichten in diesem Büchlein lassen sich spielen. Wenn man sie zu einem Hörspiel oder Theaterstück umarbeiten möchte, sind eine Reihe von Einzelschritten nötig. Am Beispiel der ersten Geschichte, "Harry's Dog", könnt ihr lernen, welche Schritte bei einer solchen Umarbeitung eingehalten werden müssen. Diese Schritte könnt ihr dann auf die anderen Erzählungen anwenden.

**1. Schritt**
Sucht die Personen heraus und beschreibt sie.

**Beispiel:**
*Harry is a boy. He's twelve years old and a pupil. He has got a dog. Its name is Barney. Harry loves Barney.*

**Nützliche Ausdrücke:**
*... is a girl/boy/woman/man.*
*... is ... years old.*
*... lives in ...*
*... is/has got/likes/doesn't like ...*
*... is X's mother/father/sister/brother/aunt/uncle/friend/...*

**Aufgabe:**
Findet alle Personen der Geschichte heraus und beschreibt sie so genau wie möglich.

**2. Schritt**
Bevor man eine Geschichte bearbeiten kann, muss man feststellen, ob die Handlung an einem oder mehreren Schauplätzen spielt und ob sie sich in verschiedene Abschnitte oder Szenen unterteilen lässt.
Diese Unterteilungen sollte man dann so genau wie möglich beschreiben.

**Beispiel:**
*The first scene is from page 4, line 2–15.*
*Harry and his dog are alone in the woods. They're eating sausages.*

*The second scene is from page 4, line 16, to page 5, line 15.*
*Harry is shouting and wants to go home, but Barney doesn't come. He's barking, he has got other ideas.*

*The third scene is from page 5, line 16–35.*
*Harry and Barney are on the bus. Barney is barking, and the other people on the bus don't like Barney.*

**Nützliche Wörter:**

| | |
|---|---|
| *page* = Seite | *section* = Abschnitt |
| *line* = Zeile | *scene* = Szene |

**Aufgabe:**
Teilt den Rest der Geschichte in verschiedene Abschnitte oder Szenen ein und beschreibt sie. Versucht, für jeden Abschnitt eine passende Überschrift zu finden.

**3. Schritt**
Überlegt, ob sich wirklich alle Abschnitte für eine Umarbeitung zu einem Hörspiel oder Theaterstück eignen.
Da Hörspiele und Theaterstücke fast nur aus Dialogen bestehen, lassen sich die Abschnitte, in denen viel wörtliche Rede (Gespräche) vorkommt, besonders gut umarbeiten.

**Aufgabe:**
Entscheidet, welche Abschnitte der Geschichte für eine Bearbeitung geeignet sind. Wie ihr seht, enthält der zweite Abschnitt nur dann wörtliche Rede, wenn Harry mit seinem Hund spricht. Daraus lässt sich aber kein interessanter Dialog machen, denn Barney kann als Antwort nur bellen. Eine Möglichkeit ist, den Abschnitt in dem Hörspiel oder Theaterstück von einem Erzähler/einer Erzählerin lesen zu lassen.

**4. Schritt**
Wenn ihr Abschnitte mit wörtlicher Rede zu einem Dialog umarbeitet, lasst ihr zunächst alles Erzählte weg. Übrig bleibt die wörtliche Rede. Wollt ihr euer Stück vortragen, müsst ihr überlegen, wie jemand etwas sagt (z. B. laut oder leise, schnell oder langsam, nachdenklich, mit ärgerlicher oder ruhiger Stimme usw.) und wie er sich dabei fühlt (z. B. glücklich, traurig, enttäuscht, beschämt usw.). Diese Beschreibung nennt man Regieanweisung.

**Beispiel:**
Page 6, line 11–20, and page 7, line 1–4:
Harry [unhappy]: *Where can he be?*
Mrs Peel [sad]: *Oh dear.*
Harry [thoughtful]: *Poor Barney. Where is he? What can I do?*
Harry to Mr Peel [anxious]: *I can't understand it, Dad. Where can he be? I hope he's all right.*

Mr Peel [quiet]: *Tell me everything.*
Mr Peel [thoughtful]: *Hmm.*
Mr Peel [quickly]: *Harry, let's go back to the woods.*
Harry [unsure]: *To the woods? Do you think ...?*
Mr Peel [unsure]: *I don't know. Let's go and see.*

**Nützliche Wörter:**

*aggressive* = aggressiv
*angry* = ärgerlich
*annoyed* = verärgert
*anxious* = besorgt
*ashamed* = beschämt
*bored* = gelangweilt
*carefully* = vorsichtig
*curious* = neugierig
*disappointed* = enttäuscht
*excited* = aufgeregt
*friendly* = freundlich
*glad* = froh
*happy* = glücklich
*loud* = laut
*pleased* = erfreut
*puzzled* = verwirrt
*quickly* = schnell
*quiet* = ruhig, leise
*rude* = unhöflich
*sad* = traurig
*shocked* = schockiert
*slowly* = langsam
*surprised* = überrascht
*thoughtful* = nachdenklich
*unhappy* = unglücklich
*unsure* = unsicher

**Aufgabe:**
Arbeitet in Gruppen. Jede Gruppe schreibt einen Abschnitt zu einem Dialog um und versucht, für jede Aussage ein passendes Wort zu finden.

**5. Schritt**
Wenn ihr die Geschichte als Theaterstück aufführen wollt, müßt ihr euch überlegen, wie sich die Schauspieler auf der Bühne verhalten sollen: wann sie auf die Bühne kommen und wann sie abtreten, wo sie gerade stehen, wie sie sich bewegen usw. Auch diese Angaben gehören zu den Regieanweisungen.

**Beispiel:**
(Harry comes into the room. His mother is sitting and reading the newspaper.)
Harry [unhappy]: *Where can he be?*
(He looks out of the window.)
Mrs Peel [sad]: *Oh dear.*
(She puts the newspaper away and goes to her son.)
Harry [thoughtful]: *Poor Barney. Where is he? What can I do?*
(Mr Peel comes into the room.)
Harry to Mr Peel [anxious]: *I can't understand it, Dad. Where can he be? I hope he's all right.*
Mr Peel [quiet]: *Tell me everything.*
(Harry tells him everything.)
Mr Peel [thoughtful]: *Hmm.*
(Mr Peel suddenly goes to the door.)
Mr Peel [quickly]: *Harry, let's go back to the woods.*
(Harry looks at his father. He doesn't understand him.)
Harry [unsure]: *To the woods? Do you think ...?*
Mr Peel [unsure]: *I don't know. Let's go and see.*

**Aufgabe:**
Arbeitet wieder in Gruppen und ergänzt bei euren Dialogen die Regieanweisungen.
Ihr könnt die Dialoge auch untereinander austauschen und für den Dialog einer anderen Gruppe die Regieanweisungen schreiben.

**6. Schritt**
Ihr habt sicher gemerkt, dass die Dialoge im Text manchmal nicht vollständig sind. Oft sind Teile des Gespräches, die man sich denken kann, ausgelassen.
Ihr könnt nun die fehlenden Teile selber ergänzen und damit eine richtige Szene schreiben.

**Beispiel:**
(Harry comes into the room. His mother is sitting and reading the newspaper.)
Harry: **Hallo, Mum. Is Barney here?**
Mrs Peel [surprised]: **No, he isn't. What's wrong?**
Harry [quickly]: **I was with him in the woods. I lost him.**
[unhappy]: *Where can he be?*
Mrs Peel [sad]: *Oh dear.*
(She puts the newspaper away and goes to her son.)
Mrs Peel [friendly]: **Don't be unhappy. Perhaps Barney can find his way home.**
Harry [thoughtful]: *Poor Barney. Where is he? What can I do?*
(Mr Peel comes into the room.)
Mr Peel [friendly]: **Hallo, everybody.**
Harry and Mrs Peel: **Barney isn't here.**
Mr Peel [unsure]: **What?**
Harry to Mr Peel [anxious]: *I can't understand it, Dad. Where can he be? I hope he's all right.*
Mr Peel [quiet]: *Tell me everything.*
Harry [quiet]: **I was in the woods with Barney. He didn't want to go home. On the bus he barked all the time. People were angry with him. Then in the street he tried to get away. I dropped him and he ran. I couldn't catch him.** (He looks at his parents.): **Where did he run to?**
Mr Peel [thoughtful]: *Hmm.*
(Mr Peel suddenly goes to the door.)
Mr Peel [quickly]: *Harry, let's go back to the woods.*
(Harry looks at his father. He doesn't understand him.)
Harry [unsure]: *To the woods? Do you think …?*
Mr Peel [unsure]: *I don't know. Let's go and see.*

**7. Schritt**
Überlegt nun in jeder Gruppe,
a) was für Kostüme die Personen tragen,
b) welche Gegenstände ihr für die einzelnen Szenen auf der Bühne braucht (diese Dinge nennt man Requisiten),
c) welche Hintergrundgeräusche ihr bei einem Hörspiel erzeugen könntet.

**Beispiele:**
a) *Harry is wearing a red polo shirt, blue jeans and black shoes. Mr Peel is wearing a police uniform. Mrs Peel is wearing pink trousers and a black blouse.*

b) *The Peels' room. There is a table and some chairs. Mrs Peel has got a newspaper. There are some plants by the window.*

*c) Wenn Harry nach Hause kommt, hört man das Klappen einer Tür, später das Rascheln von Mrs Peels Zeitung und die Schritte von Mr Peel.*

Versucht, mit wenigen Gegenständen auszukommen. So könnt ihr z. B. den Wald mit ein paar Bäumen an die Tafel zeichnen.

**8. Schritt**
Natürlich könnt ihr auch überlegen, ob ihr den einen oder anderen Dialog noch mehr erweitern oder ganz neu schreiben wollt. Ihr könnt einzelne Szenen ergänzen oder weitere Szenen schreiben. Auch Personen könnt ihr noch dazu erfinden.

**Beispiel:**
Der letzte Absatz lässt sich sehr gut zu einer Szene umschreiben.